REAL ESTATE
REAL PROFIT

The practical guide to start, make deals, manage cash-flow and build your own successful real estate empire.

by

Richard Draper

prohibited and any storage of this document is not allowed unless with written permission from the publisher. All rights reserved.

The information provided herein is stated to be truthful and consistent, in that any liability, in terms of inattention or otherwise, by any usage or abuse of any policies, processes, or directions contained within is the solitary and utter responsibility of the r ecipient reader. Under no circumstances will any l egal responsibility or blame b e held against the publisher for any reparation, damages, or monetary loss due to the information herein, either directly or indirectly.

Respective authors own all copyrights not held by the publisher.

The information herein is offered for informational purposes solely, and is universal as so. The presentation of the information is without contract or any type of guarantee assurance. The trademarks that are used are without any consent, and the publication of the trademark is without permission or backing by the trademark owner. All trademarks and brands within this book are for clarifying purposes only and are the owned by the owners themselves, not affiliated with this document.

Disclaimer and Terms of Use: The Author and Publisher has strived to be as accurate and complete as possible in the creation of this book, notwithstanding the fact that he does not warrant or represent at any time that the contents within are accurate due t o the rapidly changing nature of the Internet. While all attempts h ave been made t o v erify information provided in this publication, the Author and Publisher assumes no responsibility for errors, omissions, or contrary interpretation of the subject matter herein.

Any perceived slights of specific persons, peoples, or organizations are unintentional. In practical advice books, like anything else in life, there are no guarantees of results. Readers are cautioned to rely on their own judgment about their individual circumstances and act accordingly.

This book is not intended for use as a source of legal, medical, business, accounting or financial advice. All readers are advised to seek services of competent professionals in the legal, medical, business, accounting, and finance fields.

TABLE OF CONTENTS

CHAPTER ONE

Real Estate Real Definition

WHAT IS 'REAL ESTATE'

Real estate is property comprised of land and the buildings on it as well as the natural resources of the land including uncultivated flora and fauna, farmed crops and livestock, water and minerals. Although media often refers to the "real estate market" from the perspective of residential living, real estate can be grouped into three broad categories based on its use: residential, commercial and industrial. Examples of residential real estate include undeveloped land, houses, condominiums, and townhomes; examples of commercial real estate are office buildings, warehouses, and retail store buildings; and examples of industrial real estate are factories, mines, and farms.

Earth is the best investment on earth.

Land is the only asset you can invest in, where its value will almost always appreciate. Indeed, real estate has proved to be an avenue for creating wealth. Whether it is building your retirement home or buying plots as a group, many of us have dreamt of investing in property at a certain point in our lives. However, sometimes investing in real estate can be intimidating for beginners due to fear of the unknown.

It explains that these reservations are legitimate as he has seen people lose millions of dollars and go bankrupt overnight in real estate deals gone awry.

For smart investors who consult widely and seek guidance from professionals, the industry sure is lucrative, as we have facilitated deals in which people have made millions of dollars overnight.

CHAPTER TWO

HOW TO GET STARTED

TIPS

1. START SMALL, START NOW

A common truism in property circles is that, with real estate, you don't wait to buy, you buy and wait. Many people lose out on making a fortune because they think the money they have is too insignificant to get them into the real estate business. They don't know that there are investment packages and opportunities they can exploit if they seek guidance from a real estate agent.

To drive the point home, a scenario of two individuals with USD 100,000 each was given, and who both want to own a home in 10 years. While individual A might think it is better to save until he can raise the capital required to build a home, individual B, who gets into a joint land-buying venture with his USD 100,000, will be better off as his stake in the venture will have risen over the years since the value of land always appreciates.

There are many financing options available to people with an interest in the real estate, ranging from bank loans to mortgages and micro-finance savings packages.

Just make sure the income or appreciation value of your property surpasses the interest on the loan to avoid burning your fingers. You don't need to buy an apartment complex right out of the gate. It is okay to start small, even if it is with REITs or partnerships. Just start.

2. REAL ESTATE IS NOT A GET-RICH-QUICK SCHEME

Most people find the allure of buying property today and selling it after a short time hard to resist. However, the two professionals caution against getting into real estate with such an attitude because, like any other investment, there is always an element of risk involved.

One virtue that will prove very vital in this business is patience, which goes hand in hand with the principle of delayed gratification. A person seeking to make a fortune in the real estate sector should be prepared to work hard and learn over a long time to understand how the market works.

3. DO NOT QUIT YOUR REGULAR JOB JUST YET

If you are looking to getting started in the property sector, quitting your regular job might not be a very sound move, especially if it is the job that provided the initial capital for your investment.

According to research, people who quit their jobs to concentrate on real estate are oblivious of the fact that they can get professionals to handle the management part of their investments.

Property agents and land economists have obviously been in the industry much longer, and are thus more experienced in competently managing your investments. Relying on professionals saves you time as it only requires you to play a supervisory role.

4. DO NOT UNDERSTATE THE IMPORTANCE OF DUE DILIGENCE

The average American looking to get into real estate is always paranoid. This is because cases of people buying land whose title deeds are later revoked are rampant in many parts of the country. We have had people asking us to do a title deed verification when their investments have already gone up in smoke.

By then it is too late, and there is little we can do. To avoid being sucked into such unscrupulous deals, we advise land buyers to consult professionals , who will carry out due diligence to verify the legitimacy of the property in question.

Even when buying property from a family member, a friend or a person you think you know very well, resist the temptation to skip carrying out due diligence as unforeseen circumstances could later lead to life-long scarring.

We know of people who spend the rest of their lives servicing loans for properties that turned out to be phony. Given the kind of emotions land issues raise, it is certainly better to be safe than sorry.

5. SURROUND YOURSELF WITH THE RIGHT TEAM

When getting started, it is advisable to build a team of professionals you can easily consult before making any move, especially one that involves high financial expenditure. A property valuer, a conveyancer, an accredited contractor and a loan adviser are a few of the professionals whose advice you cannot afford to shrug off.

6. BUY THE WORST HOUSE IN THE BEST NEIGHBOURHOOD

The importance of location in any real estate investment cannot be over emphasised.

This is because property in prime locations is measured not so much by the cost of construction, but by the value and high appreciation rate of the land on which the property sits. Investing in a simple establishment in a high-end neighbourhood always pays handsomely.

However, the reverse can be the worst mistake an investor could ever make. Buying the best house in the worst neighbourhood, he warns, will always turn out to be disastrous as the value of the land underneath hardly appreciates, and future buyers will most likely shun the property because of the neighbourhood.

7. BEAR IN MIND THE 1 PER CENT RULE

When putting up commercial or residential property to let, seek advice from your agent and do your calculation in such a way that, when the property is finally ready for occupation, the money collected as monthly rent is always more than 1 per cent of the total investment cost. This is what is referred to as the 1 per cent rule.

Say you put up rental apartments at a cost of USD 1 million. The total monthly rent collected from an apartment should always be at least USD 10,000. This will enable you to recoup your investment in less than 10 years. However, the 1 per cent rule is not cast in stone.

Some investors recoup the principal investment in a shorter time, even four to six years. But those whose buildings on prime land in places such as Westlands and Kilimani take as long as 30 years.These investors rest easy knowing that the land on which their buildings sit is gaining value at a much higher rate than the rents.

8. GOOD BOOK-KEEPING WILL SAVE YOU A FORTUNE

Research points out that many small-scale constructors do not appreciate the value of accounting for every dollar spent while constructing.They thus end up getting duped by unscrupulous foremen and contractors, so building a house ends up feeling like pouring money into a bottomless pit.

It advises that investors get into the habit of keeping all the financial records pertaining to the construction.This is useful in determining the amount of rent to be charged, or the price of the building, were it to be put up for sale. Keeping records can also save you money when the time comes to file your tax returns with the Revenue Authority (RA). The financial records put you in a good position to enjoy tax exemptions.

9. DO NOT FALL IN LOVE WITH THE PROPERTY

When buying property for resale, you are better off checking your emotions at the door. There are buildings put up for sale that are over-designed and over-decorated.These buildings have great curb-appeal, that is, they look appealing at a glance. People tend to fall in love with such buildings and hence end up paying inflated prices, only for them to get shocked when they later cannot sell the building at a profit.

Clients are advised that real estate is not a sentimental business. One should always be on the lookout for profits and not let the visual appeal of a property cloud their judgment.

However, when buying your own home, you can go ahead and fork top dollar for a property with great curb appeal.

10. AVOID THE PATH OF LEAST RESISTANCE

The temptation to cut corners to save some money will certainly arise at some point. The agents agree that taking shortcuts is rarely ever worth it; if anything, it usually results in the loss of entire investments,and sometimes even lives. Going by the book might seem expensive, but it saves you a lot of mental agony and is actually cheaper.

Hire only contractors accredited and licensed by the National Construction Authority.

Take note of the national construction regulations and county by-laws to avoid the possibility of your property being demolished in future. Conduct surveys to avoid encroaching on public land, and use only genuine materials while constructing.

I have seen entire buildings being marked as unfit just because the owners did not see the need to conduct the necessary inspections at the foundation stage.

CHAPTER THREE

WHY SHOULD I INVEST IN REAL ESTATE?

Real Estate Can Provide Much Better Yields Compared to Other Investments

For most of the 1990s, the Standard & Poor's Index posted earning yields of 5 to 6 percent on average. At the same time, the S&P's dividend yields were only around 2 percent or less. Since dividend paying stocks tend to be much less volatile, the gains on the appreciation side would not normally be a significant factor. At the same time, bond yields taken as a composite, showed only around 5 percent returns. Better yields were riskier, while safer bonds returned lower yields.

The Rise of Real Estate

During the same time period and well into the 21st century, real estate investors have realized attractive returns due to the multiple income streams from real estate investments. Here is a look at some of the reasons why real estate can be beneficial for your investment portfolio:

Rental yield - This is the percentage yield from direct rental income, it and can be calculated as either gross or net. Experienced investors prefer to calculate the net rental yield—calculation detailed here—which takes the expenses, taxes and other costs into account, and divides by the property value/cost. It could be a negative cash flow, as it doesn't take mortgage payments into account. For this reason, many investors prefer to look at cash-on-cash rental yields. The example at the link shows a 6.4 percent example return on investment (ROI). Though the investor can purchase and manage for a yield on this single component that exceeds average stock or bond dividend yields, it is only one of the ways in which real estate returns on investment.

Appreciation - Rental properties normally appreciate in value with inflation. Increased value can mean sale and reinvestment in higher value properties, or provide an equity line of credit to use for other investments. This is the second, and a historically proven, value component of real estate investment return.

Inflation-proof investment - Rents usually increase with inflation, while mortgage payments on the property remain stable. This increases cash flow, without the increased expense for holding the property. When inflation goes up, it can also mean more renters as mortgages become more expensive for average consumers. More renters increase demand, so rents can escalate.

Leverage - Using leverage, while being careful to buy properties with good rental yields, provides greater returns. Using $100,000 in leveraged assets to purchase three properties with down payments, instead of one for $100,000 cash, can greatly increase returns. Of course, all leverage involves risk, so the successful investor must understand how leverage impacts their real estate investments.

Paying down loans - Amortization, or paying down loans, frees up more investment resources to increase leverage. Some investors use increased equity in one property to free up funds to invest in others.

Property improvement for equity - Many investors intentionally purchase properties at a value price, because they lack certain features or could use improvements. They have calculated that the value of the improvements will exceed the cost, resulting in an immediate increase in equity. Get more information on ARV, or after repair value.

While stocks and bonds are inflation-sensitive—and they typically involve only value appreciation potential and low or non-existent dividend/interest returns—real estate provides multi-faceted investment returns.

CHAPTER FOUR

REASONS WHY NOW IS A GREAT TIME TO INVEST IN REAL ESTATE – BUYER'S MARKET

But thanks to the same recession that caused the real estate mess, there are loads of opportunities for those with the financial resources and means to buy real estate.

1. Mortgage Interest Rates Are Low Again

Several years back when the mortgage rates hit an all-time low, people went crazy buying homes and investment properties. Some of the same people ended up getting greedy and borrowed against their newfound equity, which eventually contributed to the downturn of the real estate market. Don't repeat these mistakes.

2. The High Volume of Recent Foreclosures

Many former homeowners have been displaced due to foreclosure, so there are a lot more renters in the market, making it optimal for investors to buy rental properties without the burden of the mortgage payment.

3. People Prefer Houses to Apartments

Right or wrong, there is often a stigma associated with finding an apartment for rent. If someone has owned a home, they might see it as a step backwards to move into an apartment. This creates a great opportunity for you as a real estate investor. Also, those who have owned homes prior generally will make better tenants because they tend to treat rental homes as they are used to treating their own home.

4. Tenants Often Prefer Private Landlords

I believe most people would prefer to rent from a good private landlord as opposed to a property management company. For some, it is the security of knowing that only your landlord has the key to your home. Others might feel that there is an opportunity to eventually purchase the home through a lease with option to buy, or lease-purchase contract.

If you have a short-term investment strategy and can buy the property at a low enough price, a lease purchase or lease with option arrangement with your tenant might make sense. It also increases the likelihood that the tenant will keep the place in good shape since they are going to buy it.

5. Real Estate Prices Are at a Low

In many markets, real estate is pretty cheap. Some of the best places to buy are Arizona, Florida, California, Michigan, and Nevada. Considering that housing is generally your biggest expense, you might want to consider relocating to an area where you can get a nice property for a reasonable price. When I moved to Arizona from Maryland, my housing payment was cut by 66%, although we did also downsize our home a little.

6. The Short Sale Market

The short sale market in many areas has also created some great opportunities for getting a non-foreclosure home at a great price. In my opinion, a short sale is a better option than buying a foreclosure, because you never know what the history of the house is or what has happened while it has been sitting vacant.

7. Real Estate is a Great Long-Term Investment

Regardless of the recent crisis, real estate is still a good, long-term investment. If you look back 30 years, real estate is still valued much higher than it was. And if you have tenants paying your mortgage, it makes the investment that much more profitable.

Final Word - If you do decide to invest, meet with a trusted local real estate agent who can help you navigate the ever changing landscape of the real estate market. They often know when properties are about to go on the market and may have a lead on a short sale property that can be a great buy.

CHAPTER FIVE

REAL ESTATE INVESTING PROS AND CONS

Real Estate Investing Pros and ConsAlthough it's debatable whether real estate investing is superior or inferior to stock market investing, what isn't debatable is that real estate provides a multitude of ways to make money in the long run. There are many reasons to choose real estate investing over stock market investing, and many reasons not to. Personally I believe both are great investments, as diversification is one of my investing rules to success. Have said that, here are some of the major pros and cons of real estate investing:

Pros of Real Estate Investing

A Tangible Asset

Real estate is a tangible form of investing; You invest in properties, and you can physically see and feel your investment. This is somewhat of a luxury, as you can rest easy knowing at the end of the day that your investment isn't going anywhere (unless it's a mobile home of course). With stock market investing, you only have a computer screen showing you what you own... unless you request to have hard copies of your shares.

True Value No Matter The Economic Health

When it comes down to it, no matter if you overpaid for a property or got a great price, you still own a piece of property. Real estate will always have value, even in the worst of times because real estate is one of our basic needs. People need homes to live in, businesses need places to conduct business, and real estate will always be in demand for that reason. This doesn't mean you can't lose money in real estate, but it does mean that if you hold a piece of real estate free and clear, you own an asset with true value.

Efficient Markets Don't Truly Exist

With real estate investing you don't really have efficient markets, or markets with true transparency like you do with the stock market. What I mean by this is that you can't just easily come up with a value for a property; You can do your due diligence and reach an estimated fair value price, but it just doesn't compare to the kind of research and information available on the stock market. This is a good thing though, as inefficient markets present great opportunities for bargain priced deals. Sometimes people just don't know what is the right price to sell at, other times people are desperate and price their property extremely low. If you are familiar with your local real estate market you can easily identify these deals and invest in them.

Cons of Real Estate Investing

Not Liquid At All

Unlike the stock market, real estate investing is not a quick buy and sell atmosphere. Even if you bought a property and had a buyer lined up for it the next day, closing the deal would still take about a month on average. This can be a problem if you need liquid cash immediately, and it's a definite disadvantage compared to stock market investing.

Steep Learning Curve

In real estate you have to be knowledgeable in many different ways, and you have to have experience (or the ability to learn quickly) to overcome many little oversights or difficulties that will often come up. Knowledge is required in every sub category of real estate: mortgages, titles, insurance, construction, negotiations, market familiarity, appreciation potential, income potential, etc.. you have to be somewhat of a jack of all trades if you want to invest properly or it could cost you everything.

Significant Liabilities

If you own shares of a publicly traded company, you are not held responsible for the company's actions and thus cannot be held liable for any illegal activities. However with real estate investing, you are pretty much a target for the sue-happy type. You'll need insurance to protect yourself from the shady tenants who try and reach in your pockets, or when someone accidentally hurts themselves on your property that was entirely their own fault.

CHAPTER SIX

A NEW INVESTOR'S GUIDE TO THE TYPES OF REAL ESTATE INVESTMENTS

There are many different types of real estate investments new investors may not even realize exist. These include commercial real estate, residential real estate, industrial real estate, REITs, and more. This article will help you understand the basics.

There are many different types of real estate investments new investors may not even realize exist. These include commercial real estate, residential real estate, industrial real estate, REITs, and more. This will help you understand the basics.

Real estate is one of the oldest and most popular asset classes. Most new investors in real estate know that, but what they don't know is how many different types of real estate investments exist. It goes without saying that each type of real estate investment has its own potential benefits and pitfalls, including unique quirks in cash flow cycles, lending traditions, and standards of what is considered appropriate or normal, so you'll want to study them well before you start adding them to your portfolio.

As you uncover these different types of real estate investments and learn more about them, it isn't unusual to see someone build a fortune by learning to specialize in a particular niche. If you decide this is an area in which you might want to devote significant time, effort, and resources to in your own quest for financial independence and passive income, I'd like to walk you through some of the different kinds of real estate investing so you can get a general lay of the land.

Before we dive into the different types of real estate investments that may be available to you, I need to take a moment to explain that you should almost never buy investment real estate directly in your own name. There are a myriad of reasons, some having to do with personal asset protection. If something goes wrong and you find yourself facing something unthinkable like a lawsuit settlement that exceeds your insurance coverage, you and your advisors need the ability to put the entity that holds the real estate into bankruptcy so you have a chance to walk away to fight another day.

A major tool in structuring your affairs correctly involves the choice of legal entity. Virtually all experienced real estate investors use a special legal structure known as a Limited Liability Company, or LLC for short, or a Limited Partnership, or LP for short. You should seriously speak with your attorney and accountant about doing the same.

It can save you unspeakable financial hardship down the road. Hope for the best, plan for the worst. These special legal structures can be setup for only a few hundred dollars, or if you use a reputable attorney in a decent sized city, a few thousand dollars. The paperwork filing requirements aren't overwhelming and you could use a different LLC for each real estate investment you owned. This technique is called "asset separation" because, again, it helps protect you and your holdings. If one of your properties gets into trouble, you may be able to put it into bankruptcy without hurting the others (as long as you didn't sign an agreement to the contrary, such as a promissory note that cross-collateralized your liabilities).

With that out of the way, let's get into the heart of this book and focus on the different types of real estate.

From Apartment Buildings to Storage Units, You Can Find the Type of Real Estate Project That Appeals to Your Personality and Resources

If you're intent on developing, acquiring, or owning, or flipping real estate, you can better come to an understanding of the peculiarities of what you're facing by dividing real estate into several categories.

Residential real estate investments are properties such as houses, apartment buildings, townhouses, and vacation houses where a person or family pays you to live in the property. The length of their stay is based upon the rental agreement, or the agreement they sign with you, known as the lease agreement. Most residential leases are on a twelve-month basis in the United States.

Commercial real estate investments consist mostly of things like office buildings and skyscrapers. If you were to take some of your savings and construct a small building with individual offices, you could lease them out to companies and small business owners, who would pay you rent to use the property. It isn't unusual for commercial real estate to involve multi-year leases. This can lead to greater stability in cash flow, and even protect the owner when rental rates decline, but if the market heats up and rental rates increase substantially over a short period of time, it may not be possible to participate as the office building is locked into the old agreements.

Industrial real estate investments can consist of everything from industrial warehouses leased to firms as distribution centers over long-term agreements to storage units, car washes and other special purpose real estate that generates sales from customers who temporarily use the facility. Industrial real estate investments often have significant fee and service revenue streams, such as adding coin-operated vacuum cleaners at a car wash, to increase the return on investment for the owner.

Retail real estate investments consist of shopping malls, strip malls, and other retail storefronts. In some cases, the landlord also receives a percentage of sales generated by the tenant store in addition to a base rent to incentivize them to keep the property in top-notch condition.

Mixed-use real estate investments are those that combine any of the above categories into a single project. I know of an investor in California who took several million dollars in savings and found a mid-size town in the Midwest. He approached a bank for financing and built a mixed-use three-story office building surrounded by retail shops. The bank, which lent him the money, took out a lease on the ground floor, generating significant rental income for the owner. The the other floors were leased to a health insurance company and other businesses. The surrounding shops were quickly leased by a Panera Bread, a membership gym, a quick service restaurant, an upscale retail shop, a virtual golf range, and a hair salon. Mixed-use real estate investments are popular for those with significant assets because they have a degree of built-in diversification, which is important for controlling risk.

Beyond this, there are other ways to invest in real estate if you don't want to actually deal with the properties yourself. Real estate investment trusts, or REITs, are particularly popular in the investment community. When you invest through a REIT, you are buying shares of a corporation that owns real estate properties and distributes practically all of its income as dividends. Of course, you have to deal with some tax complexity - your dividends aren't eligible for the low tax rates you can get on common stocks - but, all in all, they can be a good addition to the right investor's portfolio if purchased at the right valuation and with a sufficient margin of safety. You can even find a REIT to match your particular desired industry; e.g,. if you want to own hotels, you can invest in hotel REITs.

You can also get into more esoteric areas, such a tax lien certificates. Technically, lending money for real estate is also considered real estate investing but I think it is more appropriate to consider this as a fixed income investment, just like a bond, because you generating your investment return by lending money in exchange for interest income. You have no underlying stake in the appreciation or profitability of a property beyond that interest income and the return of your principal.

Likewise, buying a piece of real estate or a building and then leasing it back to a tenant, such as a restaurant, is more akin to fixed income investing rather than a true real estate investment. You are essentially financing a property, although this somewhat straddles the fence of the two because you will eventually get the property back and presumably the appreciation belongs to you.

CHAPTER SEVEN

ADVANTAGES OF REAL ESTATE INVESTING

Investing in real estate is as advantageous and as attractive as investing in the stock market. I would say it has three times more prospects of making money than any other business. But, But, But... since, it is equally guided by the market forces; you cannot undermine the constant risks involved in the real estate. Let me begin discussing with you the advantages of real estate investments. I found the advantages as most suited and really practical.

Advantages

Real Estate Investments are Less Risky

As compared to other investments, less of misadventure is involved in a real estate property. I will not get away from the fact that just like any investment you make; you have the risk of losing it. Real estate investments are traditionally considered a stable and rich gainer, provided if one takes it seriously and with full sagacity. The reasons for the real estate investments becoming less risky adventure primarily relate to various socio-economic factors, location, market behavior, the population density of an area; mortgage interest rate stability; good history of land appreciation, less of inflation and many more. As a rule of thumb, if you have a geographical area where there are plenty of resources available and low stable mortgage rates, you have good reason for investing in the real estate market of such a region. On the contrary, if you have the condo in a place, which is burgeoning under the high inflation, it is far-fetched to even think of investing in its real estate market.

Not a time taking Adventure

Real estate investment will not take out all your energies, until you are prepared and foresighted to take the adventure in full swing. You can save hell lot of time, if you are vigilant enough to know the techniques of making a judicious investment in the right time and when there are good market conditions prevailing at that point of time.

You should be prepared to time yourself. Take some time out, and do market research. Initiate small adventures that involve negotiating real estate deals, buying a property, managing it and then selling it off. Calculate the time invested in your real estate negotiation. If the time was less than the optimum time, you have done it right. And if you end up investing more time, then you need to work it out again, and make some real correction for consummating next deals. You have various ways and methodologies, called the Real Estate Strategies that can make it happen for you in the right manner.

Leverage is the Right Way

The concept of leverage in real estate is not a new one. It implies investing a part of your money and borrowing the rest from other sources, like banks, investment companies, finance companies, or other people's money (OPM). There have been many instances where people have become rich by practically applying OPM Leverage Principal. As discussed under the sub head - No Need for Huge Starting Capital, the high ratio financing scheme gives an opportunity of no risk to the lenders, as the property becomes the security. Moreover, in case the lender is interested in selling the property, the net proceeds resulting from the sale of the property should comfortably cover the mortgage amount.

Now consider a situation, where the lender leverages the property at too high ratio debt say 98% or even more, and all of the sudden the market shows a down turn, then both the investor as well as the lender. Hence, greater is the mortgage debt, more is the lender's risk, and it is therefore necessary that lender pays higher interest rates. The only way out to ease the risk from lender's head is to get the mortgage insured.

Real Estate Appreciation

An appreciation is an average increase in the property value over original capital investment, taking place over a period. There are some neglected real estate properties that have an appreciation below the average mark, whereas, some of the properties located in maintained geographical areas, showing high demand, have an above average appreciation. In such centrally located and high demand areas, the average appreciation can reach up to 25% in a year. I will discuss appreciation in the chapter on real estate cycles. For now, for general understanding, appreciation is what goes up.

You Make Your Equity

As you gradually pay your mortgage debts, you are creating your equity. In other words, you would be reaching to original house price on which you have no debt. Your equity is absolutely free of percentage increase in appreciation. From the investor's perspective, in real estate market, equity is the amount that is free of debt and it is the amount that an investor holds. When you sale your property, then the net money you get, after paying all the commissions and closing costs, becomes your equity. Lenders don't want to take risk by allowing a loan on over 90% of equity. Therefore, in this manner, the lenders take the safety measures in wake of their loan being defaulted.

The Federal Bankruptcy act says that all the first mortgages of over 75% of the appraised or purchase value must be covered under high-ratio insurance schemes. However, there are certain conditions, wherein, CMHC offers the purchasers of real estate property qualifying the insurance, a mortgage of up to 100% of purchase price over your principal house value. In the wake of an event where borrowers want more money from the lenders, they would ideally settle for second and the third mortgages.

Low Inflation

Inflation is the rise in the prices of the products, commodities and services, or putting it another way, it is the decrease in your capacity to buy or hire the services. Supposing, a commodity was worth $10 a decade back, will now cost $ 100 as the result of inflation. For people who have fixed salaries feel the real brunt of the dollar, as the inflation rises. In Canada, the inflation rate varies and it varies every year. There was a time when Canada had a double-digit, but it was controlled to single digit, after the regulation of policy.

If we analyze closely, the land appreciation value for the residential real estate is 4% to 5% higher than inflation rate. Therefore, when you invest in real estate, then you are paying mortgage debts in high dollar value. Now as you are getting more, salary to pay less amount than the amount that you had paid in the original mortgage.

Tax Exemptions

You get various tax exemptions on your principal and investment income property. The tax exemptions available in real estate property investment are more than available in any other investment. In other investments, you lose terribly on the investments in your bank in the form of inflation and high taxes therein, but in real estate; you don't actually have such hindrances.

Various tax exemptions available are:

•The interest receivable from your bank account, term deposit or guaranteed Investment Certificate (GIC) is completely taxable as income. A little math here will do the magic work for you. Supposing, if you get an interest of 8% on the deposit, and the on going inflation rate is 5%, the Real Return Rate will come out to be settled at 2%.

•You get completely tax-free capital gain on principal amount of your residential real estate property.

•You have the opportunity to ward off principal amount of your residential real estate property against the home expenses incurred by you.

•You can easily ward off the property depreciation against your income.

•You can cut the expenses incurred in real estate property investment through your income

•Tax rate reduced to approx. 50% of the capital gain.

Net Positive and High Income is Generated

If taken in right direction and played seriously, a real estate investment can be your virtue making endeavor now and in times to come. You will not only be having additional assets building in your favor, but also with positive cash flow, your real estate property value will increase automatically.

High Return on Investments (ROIs)

Real estate investment gives you potentially high ROIs before and after the taxes levied on your income. In fact, investing in real estate gives you high ROIs after the taxes.

Demand for the Real Estate Increases

As a natural instance, when the population of a region increases, the total usable land decreases, and this provides the impetus for high real estate prices. There are many communities that can or cannot have growth and development regulations, thereby, resulting in limited land available for use. Therefore, the real estate prices of the area shoot up. Remember housing is the necessity of an individual and therefore it is much in demand than any other single commodity taken. Furthermore, there are people who purchase additional houses for their recreation, recluse or as a past time. This in turn increases the demand for land.

CHAPTER EIGHT

THINGS YOU MUST DO TO SUCCEED AT REAL ESTATE INVESTING

Here are three simple guidelines that must be followed if you plan to succeed at real estate investing. It's not everything, of course, but at the very least, you must be willing to commit to these things if you want to become a successful real estate investor.

Acknowledge the Basics

Real estate investing involves acquisition, holding, and sale of rights in real property with the expectation of using cash inflows for potential future cash outflows and thereby generating a favorable rate of return on that investment.More advantageous then stock investments (which usually require more investor equity) real estate investments offer the advantage to leverage a real estate property heavily. In other words, with an investment in real estate, you can use other people's money to magnify your rate of return and control a much larger investment than would be possible otherwise. Moreover, with rental property, you can virtually use other people's money to pay off your loan.

But aside from leverage, real estate investing provides other benefits to investors such as yields from annual after-tax cash flows, equity buildup through appreciation of the asset, and cash flow after tax upon sale. Plus, non-monetary returns such as pride of ownership, the security that you control ownership, and portfolio diversification.

Of course, capital is required, there are risks associated with investing in real estate, and real estate investment property can be management-intensive. Nonetheless, real estate investing is a source of wealth, and that should be enough motivation for us to want to get better at it.

Understand the Elements of Return

Real estate is not purchased, held, or sold on emotion. Real estate investing is not a love affair; it's about a return on investment. As such, prudent real estate investors always consider these four basic elements of return to determine the potential benefits of purchasing, holding on to, or selling an income property investment.

1. Cash Flow - The amount of money that comes in from rents and other income less what goes out for operating expenses and debt service (loan payment) determines a property's cash flow. Furthermore, real estate investing is all about the investment property's cash flow. You're purchasing a rental property's income stream, so be sure that the numbers you rely on later to calculate cash flow are truthful and correct.

2. Appreciation - This is the growth in value of a property over time, or future selling price minus original purchase price. The fundamental truth to understand about appreciation, however, is that real estate investors buy the income stream of investment property. It stands to reason, therefore, that the more income you can sell, the more you can expect your property to be worth. In other words, make a determination about the likelihood of an increase in income and throw it into your decision-making.

3. Loan Amortization - This means a periodic reduction of the loan over time leading to increased equity. Because lenders evaluate rental property based on income stream, when buying multifamily property, present lenders with clear and concise cash flow reports. Properties with income and expenses represented accurately to the lender increase the chances the investor will obtain a favorable financing.

4. Tax Shelter - This signifies a legal way to use real estate investment property to reduce annual or ultimate income taxes. No one-size-fits-all, though, and the prudent real estate investor should check with a tax expert to be sure what the current tax laws are for the investor in any particular year.

Do Your Homework

1. Form the correct attitude. Dispel the thought that investing in rental properties is like buying a home and develop the attitude that real estate investing is business. Look beyond curb appeal, exciting amenities, and desirable floor plans unless they contribute to the income. Focus on the numbers. "Only women are beautiful," an investor once told me. "What are the numbers?"

2. Develop a real estate investment goal with meaningful objectives. Have a plan with stated goals that best frames your investment strategy; it's one of the most important elements of successful investing. What do you want to achieve? By when do you want to achieve it? How much cash are you willing to invest comfortably, and what rate of return are you hoping to generate?

3. Research your market. Understanding as much as possible about the conditions of the real estate market surrounding the rental property you want to purchase is a necessary and prudent approach to real estate investing. Learn about property values, rents, and occupancy rates in your local area. You can turn to a qualified real estate professional or speak with the county tax assessor.

4. Learn the terms and returns and how to compute them. Get familiar with the nuances of real estate investing and learn the terms, formulas, and calculations. There are sites online that provide free information.

5. Consider investing in real estate investment software. Having the ability to create your own rental property analysis gives you more control about how the cash flow numbers are presented and a better understanding about a property's profitability. There are software providers online.

6. Create a relationship with a real estate professional that knows the local real estate market and understands rental property. It won't advance your investment objectives to spend time with an agent unless that person knows about investment property and is adequately prepared to help you correctly procure it. Work with a real estate investment specialist.

CHAPTER NINE

ESSENTIAL FEATURES THAT MAKE REAL ESTATE INVESTING PROFITABLE

Every now and then persons trying to make up their minds where to put their money ask me if real estate ventures are more or less profitable, compared to other businesses opportunities around.

My response is always that apart from its potential for yielding significant profits, investing in real estate often confers long terms benefits.

You Can Refurbish (to Enhance the Value of) Real Estate

After you buy a stock, you hold it for a period of time and hopefully sell it for a profit. The success of the stock depends on company management and their corporate success, which is out of your control.

Unlike other conventional investment instruments, like stocks, for instance, whose rate of returns, depend on third parties (e.g. company management), real estate investments are directly under your control. Even though you will not be able to control changes that may occur in demographic and economic aspects, or impact of nature induced changes, there are many other aspects that you can control, to boost the returns on your investment in it.

Real Estate Investments Are Immune to Inflation

In other words, investing your money in ownership of viable real estate can protect you from the harsh effects that inflation usually has on other conventional investments. This is because the value of real estate generally tends to rise in positive correlation with inflationary pressures. This is why property values and rental rates go up with rising inflation.

The nature of real estate, therefore affords owners the unique advantage of being able to adjust the rates they offer, to match inflation.

Monthly rents for example can be raised to compensate for inflation - thus providing a cushion effect against inflation induced losses that other monetary investments suffer.

Real Estate Investing Allows Use of Other People's Money

In other words, you can do it even if you do not have enough money. You just need to know how. This is possible because real estate is physical property or what is called a hard asset. That is an attribute that makes it attractive to financiers i.e. people with money to invest.

This is why many times real estate products are bought with debt - unlike conventional investment products like stocks which are NOT tangible, and therefore perceived as being more risky to invest in. So real estate investment can be done using cash or mortgage financing. In the latter case, payments can be so arranged to allow payment of low initial sums, provided by you or a willing third party.

Those payments will be happening on landed property which will continue increasing in value throughout the duration of such payments - and indeed beyond. That further inspires confidence in the minds of those financing the acquisition, that their investment is safe.

Little wonder that real estate investing has continued to prosper for so long!

CHAPTER TEN

EASY ACTION STEPS TO A SUCCESSFUL START IN REAL ESTATE INVESTING

Here are a few detailed steps that an investor can take to improve the chances for success.

- Learn the basics of real estate in general.

As with any investment strategy or business, real estate comes with its' very own lingo. There are terms and phrases that many of us have heard in the past, yet may not know the exact meaning. It is very important from the get go to do the research and learn the basics such as the meaning of the terms and phrases that are used in the real estate industry every day. You can start by using a search engine and searching the phrase "real estate definitions".

- **Begin home study education**.

There are great benefits to home study and I do not mean the courses we eluded to on weekend cable T.V. At your local library, in the real estate investing section, there will be multiple titles recently written by authors with experience in their topic. Check out as many titles as you can read in a week and o to work reading. Write down sentences and topics that come up in the books that interest you and that fit into your reasoning for starting to invest in real estate. This will be the start of your plan for getting started.

- Develop a game plan.

By this point, you have an idea of the general terms and phrases for the property investing world and have begun to grow your interest and understanding of the specific strategies for real estate investing. It is time to formally develop your plan and start taking action. Each of the real estate investing books that you will be reading give specific advice about team building. It is a crucial step for your success and the best books offer advice about who to put on your team, where to find them and how important they are to your over-all success. Before you can start investing, you must have a plan for where you are going and how you are going to get there.

- **Join local organizations for investors.**

In every city, county and state there are multiple organizations whose missions are to assist real estate investors. Each of these organizations holds monthly meetings and some of the best even hold weekly meetings, where investors can network and learn. These meetings are crucial to a beginner investor because they offer the opportunity to build your team with experienced members. They also are fantastic groups to attend for tips, tricks and education. Join a group close to you and make your attendance mandatory. Attend as many meetings as possible each month. Often times, the simple step of surrounding yourself with like-minded individuals who are positive and re-enforce your determination to succeed, can have the biggest benefit on your future success.

- **Find partners & Do not fall for get rich quick!**

One mistake that is easy to make in the beginning is to set off on the path of "go it alone". Another is to believe that just around the corner is a pot of gold if I can just find a deal like those guys on T.V.! One thing that is seldom talked about is the fact that most real estate investors have used partnerships in the past if they are not using them now. Partnerships are a great way to spread the risk of investing while learning the ropes. Those risks include using less of your available capital, credit and time.

Partnerships can also be structured to be a simple 50/50 partnership splitting all costs and profits or a slightly more complicated partnership with one partner providing money and the other providing the deals, follow through and managing the investments. Either way, going it alone can be a lonely, long and expensive way to get started investing.

- Do not quit your day job!

This is a biggie and is a MAJOR mistake made by some first time real estate investors. Investing in real estate requires a total commitment - a "burning of the boats" mentality. There is no turning back when you decide to go all in. And in that statement lies the problem with leaving your day job first. Take time to develop your team, to build cash reserves, to learn the ropes. Take time to make small mistakes before you leave your full time employment and make a big mistake! Investing in real estate is a big picture endeavor and as an investor you have to be able to clearly see your future and plan accordingly.

These last two tips really go to the heart of why some investors not only fail, but fail miserably. Many times you can overcome the mistakes with the first few tips here by perseverance and a little luck. If you make one of the following two mistakes, they can quickly break a new investor and sour the experience for a good long time. Then again, if you follow all the previous tips, chances are you will have the team around you to guide you right past these last two tips and onto smooth investing.

- **Once started, DO NOT under estimate repairs.**

When you are estimating the repairs to a property for investment, unless you have an experienced contractor and trusted advisor on your team, you can miss the mark wildly. Even the best home study courses are not able to provide you with an accurate ability to estimate costs. It takes experience and time before you can accurately guesstimate repair costs. Missing the mark on estimated repairs can quickly break a bank account and take a property from profitable to money pit quickly!

- **Do not purchase investment property for equity or appreciation**

There is no bigger mistake an real estate investor can make today than to purchase property for its equity holding or future appreciation. Long-term investing today is centered around the ability of a property to perform with a positive monthly cash flow. In my home city for investing, Memphis, real estate investors purchase properties at extreme discounts, but over look those discounts if the property does not provide a high enough monthly cash flow. Equity and expectations of future home values are not good reasons to purchase investment property.

Many individuals will purchase their first investment property in 2010. Some will view their purchase as strictly an investment and others will look for real estate to provide a new profession. Either way, it is extremely important that first-time investors seek all of the help, advice and experience they can get from other investors.

102

CHAPTER ELEVEN

WHAT EVERY REAL ESTATE INVESTING BEGINNER NEEDS TO KNOW:

1) You will have to trade time or money to get what you want in real estate. You can't get something for nothing, so even if you buy an expensive course to get someone else's experience and shave years off your learning curve, you'll still HAVE a learning curve. Plus, you'll need to find leads, and that type of marketing takes (you guessed it) time and/or money.

2) Leverage cuts both ways. When the market is going up, leverage can be a great ally in helping you acquire more property with less of your own money. However, when the market is soft or declining, as also happens with real estate market cycles, having a lot of leverage can put you "upside down" on your equity and cash flow - a very risky situation. Protect yourself by "making your money when you buy" and passing up those "skinny" deals.

3) It's all about NEGOTIATING with the motivated sellers. A lot of courses make you believe that if you find the motivated sellers, you can just pluck up the deals like daisies in the orchard. That's almost true. Whether you're working in commercial or residential real estate, you'll get much better deals when you negotiate with a motivated seller. However, the key is that you must NEGOTIATE. You have to make offers that will work for you and engage the sellers in conversation. Very rarely will the buildings be lying these listed for 50 cents on the dollar (if they are, they'll be

snapped up by other investors). You have to find sellers that you think may be motivated and offer them your low cash offer or terms offer in order to see if they're willing to work with you. Engage them in the conversation by making lots of offers, and NEGOTIATING with the ones that are motivated.

4) Figure out your rate of return. Sometimes, when you don't have a deal, it's easy to think "any" deal would be good. However, sometimes the best deals are the ones you PASS on - you "make" your money by saving yourself from some expensive mistakes. Don't waste time on property that doesn't make sense when you run the numbers. Don't get emotionally attached just because someone says they're motivated or willing to work out terms with you. Run the numbers. Always focus on the numbers.

5) You get paid for solving problems. This is a business with a lot of problems. Sellers can get very emotional, or have a lot of financial trouble, at the time that you'll be working with them. That's stressful for anyone, especially when the transfer of a large asset like a house, apartment building or office/retail center is involved. Realize that you may go through some challenging emotions of your own. That's natural. If you can hold it together and survive the up-and-down roller coaster, you should do okay.

No one says real estate is easy unless they have a course to sell you. It can offer some great returns, but there's a reason not everyone goes after them. Not every property is a winner and finding and acquiring the winners can be a challenge. However, if you are committed to making your real estate investments work for you, then focus on getting yourself educated and staying in for the long run.

CHAPTER TWELVE

BECOMING A REAL ESTATE ENTREPRENEUR: EVERYTHING YOU NEED TO KNOW

Traditionally, there are a few ways to make serious money as an entrepreneur. They include business ownership; securities investment and speculation; and, perhaps the most personally rewarding, real estate entrepreneurship. Not for the faint of heart, making money in real estate is filled with potential challenges and pitfalls. But with an understanding of the various real estate entrepreneurship strategies, proper implementation, assessment, and adjustment where necessary, one can make substantial profits.

The first step is understanding how to make money in real estate.

1) strategies for making money with real estate,

2) determining return on investment (ROI),

3) making money with residential real estate,

4) building a business based on commercial real estate,

5) real estate financing,

6) economic trends affecting the real estate market,

7) keys to success to become a real estate entrepreneur,

8) challenges of being a real estate entrepreneur,

9) examples of real estate entrepreneurs.

STRATEGIES FOR MAKING MONEY WITH REAL ESTATE

There are a number of ways to make money in real estate, including, but not limited to:owning and renting residential property buying and selling residential property improving residential property to increase its value; investing in mortgage notes; owning and renting commercial property; buying and selling commercial property; investing in commercial real estate; and investing in real estate securities, such as real estate investment trusts (REITs) and municipal bonds.

Broadly speaking, each strategy involves determining your goals, researching your market, finding the proper asset(s), financing the purchase of the asset(s), receiving income from the asset(s) and/or selling the asset(s) at a higher price than what you have paid for it. Real estate entrepreneurs typically estimate ROI – the return on investment of the asset in question, as a way of evaluating whether it is worth purchasing.

DETERMINING ROI

ROI, in a real estate context, can be calculated in a couple of ways. The basic ROI formula for any investment is:

ROI = (Gain from investment – Cost investment)/Cost of investment

But this method does not fully incorporate costs or changes in equity. Two alternate methods are the Cost Method:

Cost Method of ROI = Equity/Costs of purchase and improvementswhich incorporates any anticipated changes in equity, and the Out-of-Pocket Method:

Out-of-Pocket Method = Equity/Costs of purchase and improvements + loan-related costs

Most real estate investors prefer the Out-of-Pocket Method. These formulas should be taken as a starting point, as they do not take into account factors like time spent on repairs, tenant management, sudden falling real estate prices, difficulties selling the property, or other unforeseen occurrences that can affect the success of failure of a real estate investment.

CHAPTER THIRTEEN

MAKING MONEY WITH RESIDENTIAL REAL ESTATE

There are a number of ways to make money in the residential real estate market, including making home improvements, flipping houses, owning and renting property, investing in residential real estate, and investing in mortgage notes.

Home Improvements

Real estate entrepreneurs often make improvements to residential properties to increase their value. They use this increased value to justify selling the property for more than they paid for it. This strategy is commonly employed when flipping houses. Sometimes, entrepreneurs will look for distressed properties – properties with liens on them, or in need of substantial repair in order to be issued a Certificate of Occupancy. The latter are known as fixer-uppers, and should be carefully assessed prior to purchase to ensure profitability.

Buying and Selling (Flipping) Houses

One of the most common ways to make money with residential property is by flipping it. this involves buying property, often at a discount to its market value, and selling it for a higher price. Frequently, once residential property has been purchased, the new owner will make improvements, designed to drive up the value. Once the entrepreneur is able to obtain an appraisal for the property substantially higher than what they paid for it (minus expenses), then they will sell it for a profit. The typical time frame is 30 to 60 days. The difficulties of obtaining a mortgage for a property other than one's primary residence can make this a high-risk strategy.

Often entrepreneurs will flock to areas in which real estate prices are rising. They may buy a residential property at or above market price, and/or at a premium to its underlying value, with the expectation that they can sell it at an even higher price. This can be a dangerous game however, as rising asset prices often are a part of an asset bubble – in this case, a real estate bubble. When the bubble bursts, it's not uncommon for investors to lose more than they paid for the property.

Owning and Renting Property

Many real estate entrepreneurs buy residential property to rent to others. Expenses can be considerable, including closing costs, maintenance and upkeep, property taxes, any existing debt, and problem tenants, among others. Because of this, this strategy makes sense when the rental income minus expenses is a net positive. This is known as a cash–flow positive property.

Once you purchase one property and build up some equity, lenders typically will lend you money for additional investment purchases (usually no more than 80% of your accrued equity).

Investing in Residential Real Estate

Other entrepreneurs buy and hold several residential real estate properties for property appreciation and rental income. Historically, in the U.S., home prices have appreciated over the long-term, and some analysts, such as Bespoke Investment Group, predict that globally, home prices will continue to appreciate over time. Some entrepreneurs purchase a property or multiple properties they feel will be appraised at a much higher value over a long time horizon (15 to 30 years or more). They may then sell those properties for a profit, keep them as a store of value, or hold onto them in the hopes of further appreciation. Long-term buy and hold strategies often involve improvements on the properties in question. Additionally, they often employ a property manager or the services of a property management firms to manage their holdings, uninterested in the day-to-day work of being a landlord. Again, these entrepreneurs look to build portfolios of properties for which the rental income minus expenses (including the services of a property manager/property management firm) is a net positive.

Investing in Mortgage Notes

Some real estate entrepreneurs buy and sell mortgage notes, to and from other investors, banks, and financial entities. The entrepreneur who owns a mortgage note owns a homeowner's mortgage debt and is entitled to the mortgage payments the homeowner might otherwise pay a bank or other mortgage originator.

BUILDING A BUSINESS BASED ON COMMERCIAL REAL ESTATE

Another way to make money in real estate is building a business based on commercial real estate. The most common is a holding company – a business entity designated as the "owner" of residential or commercial real estate property. Such an entity often provides the true owner certain tax advantages and insulates them, to a certain extent, from some forms of personal liability relating to property ownership. One can, and should, set up such an entity to buy; own and rent; and invest in commercial property.

Buying Commercial Property

Some real estate entrepreneurs seek to make their fortunes buying commercial property. Much like with residential real estate, they can do this with the intentions of making improvements on the property, driving up the value, and selling it; renting the property to commercial tenants; or holding it for price appreciation, in addition to rental income. Commercial real estate is often thought of, but is not limited to "office space"; it also can include retail storefronts; industrial buildings; multifamily apartments (usually four units or more); hotels; land; entertainment venues, such as casinos or concert halls; or sporting venues, such as stadiums or golf courses.

Owning and Renting Property

Commercial property rental income can be extremely lucrative, depending on the property, location, and tenants. A long-term lease of a retail space in a centrally located building could be worth anywhere from tens of thousands of dollars to millions of dollars per year depending on the location and size of the space.

Investing in Commercial Real Estate

Real estate entrepreneurs often invest in commercial real estate, developing portfolios of properties that not just provide lucrative rental income, but are also expected to appreciate in value over time. Many of these investors roll over the profits from their successful properties into new ones, leaving the daily management of the properties to property management firms.

Investing in Real Estate Securities

Real estate entrepreneurs can also invest in real estate securities, including, but not limited to REITs and municipal bonds. REITs are a form of limited partnership that is securitized. The limited partnership invested the monies raised from the sale of its securities on the capital markets in real estate, usually commercial. The limited partnership handles the day-to-day management of the portfolio of properties, including buying and selling them. The securities trade on the capital markets based on the market assessment of the limited partnership's value.

Municipal bonds are issued by cities and states to raise funds for a number of different municipal initiatives, including capital construction projects. By investing in the debt issued to finance the securities, you are, in essence, investing in public property. Municipal bonds often come with certain tax exemptions, which can be advantageous to bondholders.

REAL ESTATE FINANCING

Real estate purchases can be financed in any number of ways. The easiest is an outright cash purchase, for those who can afford to do so. However, -many real estate transactions are debt financed. Some entrepreneurs use home equity lines of credit, buy new homes while renting out their existing ones, or purchase duplexes or multifamily homes. It's critical to know the keys to obtain favorable loan terms, such as having a sizable down payment and a strong borrowing profile, and looking at neighborhood banking institutions and alternative lenders, such as peer-to-peer lending institutions for options and flexibility. Sometimes the property owner will even assume the note for your purchase, meaning you pay them directly, a method known as seller carry-back. A thorough understanding of real estate financing methods is critical to your success.

ECONOMIC TRENDS AFFECTING THE REAL ESTATE MARKET

Real estate entrepreneurs should be aware of a number of key trends affecting the real estate market. They include, but are not limited to:interest rates – how expensive it is to borrow money homeownership rates – a gauge of demand for primary residences; rental vacancy rates – a gauge of demand for residential rental properties; and geo-demographic shifts – where people are moving to or from.

There may be more or fewer factors at play with your planned investment, but it is critical that you know how all the key trends affect your market(s) of interest.

RICHARD DRAPER

128

CHAPTER FOURTEEN

KEYS TO SUCCESS TO BECOME A REAL ESTATE ENTREPRENEUR

Each successful entrepreneur's path is different, but there are some commonalities. Successful real estate entrepreneurs are clear about their real estate goals, often writing them down before taking any other step. They understand their market(s), because they do thorough and rigorous research. They determine their time horizon and exit strategy before entry. They put together a team of professionals to compensate for their knowledge deficiencies, including but not limited to: real estate agents, contractors, lawyers, appraisers, lenders, marketers, and accountants. And they do their due diligence.

Real estate entrepreneurs need to be tenacious. Real estate investing is not an easy thing to do and there are many people trying to do it. Successful entrepreneurs stick with their plan, adjusting it to address challenges, often setting aside a set time per week to pursue their real estate goals. It is also critical to study trends and use them to find opportunities.

CHALLENGES OF BEING A REAL ESTATE ENTREPRENEUR

In addition to the aforementioned asset bubbles, financing is one of the biggest challenges in real estate entrepreneurship. It is challenging to be successful with a less than stellar credit history, or during periods where regionally or nationally, lenders are making fewer loans.

Another challenge is finding properties that provide the proper return on investment. For one, there are many real estate investors and aspiring real estate investors. Further, many properties require substantial work, rather improvements, payment of liens, or other investments of time and money. The time required in particular may not make particular properties worth it to investors. Finding those ideal properties that, after the time and cost, provide a lucrative return requires tenacity.

Other challenges include the many variables at play. With a typical rental property – commercial or residential, a hundred things could go wrong over which the investor has little control, from inclement weather to nightmare tenants. Proper contingency planning is essential. In fact, contingency planning is one of the only things in real estate entrepreneurship over which an investor does have control.

EXAMPLES OF REAL ESTATE ENTREPRENEURS

There are many examples of successful real estate entrepreneurs, but perhaps none more visible and vocal than Donald Trump. Trump has amassed a multi-billion dollar portfolio of commercial real estate across the globe. Another is Steve Wynn, who helped revitalize the Vegas Strip, through the development and refurbishment of popular Vegas resorts, such as the Bellagio, which his company owns.

On a smaller scale, real estate entrepreneurs like Janet French, owner of SilverMoon Entities, rehab, flip, and acquire income generating properties. But not every entrepreneur makes their money through property ownership. There are a lot of steps in the process of acquisition and opportunities to make money along the way. For example, take Ankit Duggal, the founder and owner of RER, LLC, which started as a firm focused on structure short sales for homeowners facing foreclosure, and now makes money by flipping these properties. While their paths may have been different, each of these real estate entrepreneurs set goals, researched opportunities, implemented their plan, and made adjustments to overcome the challenges they encountered.

CHAPTER FIFTEEN

TIPS FOR REAL ESTATE INVESTING SUCCESS

Tip #1: Create a game plan.

Decide what you want to accomplish and outline the steps that you must take to get there. Who will be involved? How will you meet them and gain their cooperation? How much time will it take? Where will you find this time? How much will it cost, and where will you get this money? What's the risk? How will you handle it?

This plan will serve as your guide each day, so you need to get it right. That brings us to the next tip...

Tip #2: Have an expert review your plan.

The first real estate investing plan I created involved me single-handedly buying 100 houses in a year. And it listed several different marketing strategies that were completely cost ineffective. I had a friend of mine (who isn't even involved in real estate) review the plan, and he said it looked good. How silly of me!

About eight months into working this over-reaching and misguided plan, I had an expert investor review it. He tore it apart, and together we reconstructed a better plan with more realistic goals (buy 12 houses, not 100) and a more effective marketing plan.

Shortly thereafter, I bought 6 houses, and I actually felt good about my progress. Six out of twelve feels much better than six out of 100!

Tip #3: Don't give up.

The life of a new real estate investor is filled with countless highs and lows. You're on a high when you think you have a property all locked up to purchase, and then you hit a low when it suddenly falls though at closing.

Or you're on a high when you finally do close on that house, but you hit a low when you hit a 3-week dry spell and it feels like you couldn't get a seller to agree to your price--even if you paid double.

Tip #4: Take baby steps.

When you break it all down, big goals, big dreams, and big plans are nothing more than a series of miniature action steps or "to do" items. When you dissect the daily life of a successful investor, you'll find that he or she does 8 to 12 things each day that are real estate related.

One item might be "Watch DVD #5 in the new investing course ." Another item might be "Call the title company about the name on the warranty deed" or "Meet the inspector at the house on Watson Street."

All of these little tasks each day add up to what is, or what eventually will be, a large and highly profitable real estate investing operation. So don't toss that "to do" list by the wayside, thinking that your small efforts today don't mean much. They mean everything.

Tip #5 Do what you say you're going to do.

As a real estate investor, your reputation means everything. They say it's a small world, but the world of real estate investing is even smaller. So be honest, be courteous, and for heaven's sake, do what you say you're going to do. If you say you're going to buy another investor's house, by golly, you better move mountains--if that's what it takes-- to buy it!

Otherwise, your name will eventually become mud, and you'll have a tough time buying from not only that investor, but just about every other investor in town. Believe me, I can count at least 10 local investors of the top of my head who I will NOT do business with because their word means nothing. And I know several other investors who won't deal with them either. You DO NOT want to be black listed.

Tip #6: Be on time.

Showing up late is just about one of the most disrespectful things you can do to another real estate investor, inspector, contractor, or anyone for that matter. It shows them that you don't value them or their time, and time is MUCH more valuable than money. Money can be replaced. Time cannot.

When someone shows up late for a meeting with me, they instantly lose credibility. And there are countless other investors who feel the same way. On the other hand, when an investor or business associate shows up on time or early, it makes me want to smile, reach out my hand, and strike a win-win deal.

So be on time. You're much more likely to create trusted allies who can help you along your path to success.

Tip #7: Eliminate certain activities.

I'll wrap up with one more tip that is closely linked to the first tip, "Create a Game Plan." That game plan will involve a series of goals and steps or "to do" items that you must follow to become successful. But what many people don't seem to realize is that for all of these things to happen, certain activities in your current schedule must be REMOVED.

For example, if you're going to attend two real estate meetings and make five offers per week, what must go? Possibly TV time. Possibly a friendship. Possibly your workout plan. Of course, what has to go is unique to each of us, but you must realize that if you're an extremely busy person, you'll have to make some TOUGH sacrifices.

But these sacrifices are only for the short run. If you have to quit your exercise program to have enough time for real estate, for example, then so be it. You can resume in two years after you've achieved financial freedom through real estate. And you'll have more time to exercise than ever.

Early on in real estate, I gave up friendships, exercise, sleep, vacations, and leisure time. How much you give up depends on how quickly you want to become financially independent.

It can be a tough to integrate all of these tips into your daily routine at once. So for now, I encourage you to focus on the one tip that you think can benefit your investing business the most. After you've turned that tip into a habit that's part of your daily routine, then move on to the next. Keep moving forward and never give up, and you'll be a successful and financially free investor in no time!

CHAPTER SIXTEEN

TOP REAL ESTATE INVESTMENT STRATEGIES

Real estate is a huge industry and there are a lot of opportunities to invest in real estate. But where should you start? What types of real estate investing is best for you? Learning the basics of how to invest in real estate is the first step in choosing a strategy. You can then explore different real estate investment strategies and pick one based on your time, budget, and long-term goals.

Different Real Estate Investment Strategies

1) Buy and Holds

These are good long-term investments because of the steady additional income and the opportunity to gain appreciation. If looking for an active, long-term investment, buy-and-holds are the way to go.

Buying an investment property as a buy-and-hold requires research about the market, neighborhood, and property expenses. Positive cash-flow is very important with these investment because money is otherwise lost every month. With buy-and-holds, deciding on becoming a landlord or hiring property management is also something to consider. Can you manage the property yourself? Can you handle having tenants?

Not all buy-and-hold properties are the same. These can range from single-family homes to entire apartment buildings. Depending on location and cash flow, an investor might choose to rent out an entire single-family home to a family or rent out individual rooms to individual tenants. Multi-family homes are popular if the investor wants to have a personal residence at the same location as their investments. The advantage with multi-family homes is being able to spend less and gain more. Finally, apartment buildings can range from small to large buildings. When owning an apartment building, you are becoming the home owner association, and can create your own rules to follow.

2) Airbnb Investment Properties

These are also a type of buy-and-hold property but are vacation or short-term rentals. When buying an investment property as a vacation rental, there are different things to consider. Can you manage turnover between tenants? What are the occupancy rates like in your area? What are the legal regulations for having a short-term rental or Airbnb investment property?

There has been an increase in the number of Airbnb investors as Airbnb investment properties have proved to be lucrative and sometimes produce more income than traditional investments. Search for the optimal real estate investment strategies in your area to find out if traditional or Airbnb investing has higher returns.

3) Fix and Flips

Fix-and-flips are for investors looking for active, short-term investments to quickly make money. Fix-and-flips are properties that are bought, renovated, and then sold. They are not a get-rich quick scheme but if done correctly, investors can quickly profit from this strategy.

When looking for a property to flip, it's important to look for deal-breakers. After setting a budget, it's crucial to consult an inspector, contractor, and appraiser in order to identify issues and avoid losing time and money. When flipping, time is the biggest asset. The longer it takes to flip the property, the more monthly expenses.

4) Commercial

The U.S. commercial market is huge, and joining commercial real estate investing can lead to huge returns. These properties are leased to businesses which can range from tiny little stores to shopping malls. While there's an opportunity to rent out to big businesses and get significant cash flow, vacancies can last a longer than with residential properties. This strategy is not for beginners but it's a great level to reach in your real estate portfolio. Read more in the next point about how you can do this.

5) Passive Investments

Passively investing in real estate means not getting your hands dirty and giving your money to someone else to make the investment happen. One way to do this is by working with a Real Estate Investment Trust (REIT), which is when a group of investors pool their money to buy large real estate investments, such as malls, skyscrapers, or many single-family homes. Each investor gets a share of the profits and does very little work. These passive investments generally have higher returns and less risk. Different types of REITs include retail, residential, healthcare, office, and mortgage REITs. An investor can invest in a stock exchange-listed REIT or buy a share in a REIT mutual fund. It's best to consult a financial expert to see if this real estate investment strategy would for you.

Another way to passively invest in real estate is lending your money to an investor looking for a property to flip. Why wouldn't an investor just go to a bank? It's difficult to get a loan for a property that is vacant and needs work. This loan is called a first trust deed investment. The investors should pay the 20% down payment and closing costs. As a lender, you would receive interest payments on the loan and a final payment at the end of the term. You money is secured by the property.

6) Real Estate Wholesaling

Making money in real estate does not always require spending money, there are so many diverse opportunities to invest. Wholesaling is one of the ways you can create an income without having to spend any money at at all. A wholesaler finds a seller who wants to put their property up for sale and has not yet gone on the market. The wholesaler finds a buyer and then is entitled to a share of the selling price. To be successful with the real estate investment strategy, you have to network and make contacts in order to have a database of potential sellers and buyers.

Real Estate Tips

1) Research

Before deciding on any real estate investment strategies, make sure to thoroughly understand what each strategy entails. Do an investment property analysis before investing in a rental property or commercial property. Using analytics can help you find the best investment properties and neighborhoods.

2) Network and Join Real Estate Investment Clubs

Join real estate investment clubs to learn about investment strategies and to find partners to work with. Having different team members or contacts with different specialities is very beneficial. Besides getting investment tips, you can call on them when in need of a help.

3) Location, Not Convenience

It can't be said enough – location is key in real estate. Try to explore areas that will give the highest returns and avoid staying in your area just for the sake of convenience. When you have a location, you can focus on a niche market and better appeal to tenants. For example, if you decide to invest in a college town, you can focus on providing housing suitable for students.

Real estate investing offers a lot more opportunities than most investments. Once you've done enough research about different real estate investment strategies, you can have a better idea of what you want and become the investor you want to be.

CHAPTER SEVENTEEN

REAL ESTATE INVESTING

Real estate investing involves the purchase, ownership, management, rental and/or sale of real estate for profit. Improvement of realty property as part of a real estate investment strategy is generally considered to be a sub-specialty of real estate investing called real estate development. Real estate is an asset form with limited liquidity relative to other investments, it is also capital intensive (although capital may be gained through mortgage leverage) and is highly cash flow dependent. If these factors are not well understood and managed by the investor, real estate becomes a risky investment. The primary cause of investment failure for real estate is that the investor goes into negative cash flow for a period of time that is not sustainable, often forcing them to resell the property at a loss or go into insolvency. A similar practice known as flipping is another reason for failure as the nature of the investment is often associated with short term profit with less effort.

Real estate markets in most countries are not as organized or efficient as markets for other, more liquid investment instruments. Individual properties are unique to themselves and not directly interchangeable, which presents a major challenge to an investor seeking to evaluate prices and investment opportunities. For this reason, locating properties in which to invest can involve substantial work and competition among investors to purchase individual properties may be highly variable depending on knowledge of availability. Information asymmetries are commonplace in real estate markets. This increases transactional risk, but also provides many opportunities for investors to obtain properties at bargain prices.

Real estate entrepreneurs typically use a variety of appraisal techniques to determine the value of properties prior to purchase.

Typical sources of investment properties include:

Market listings (through a Multiple Listing Service or Commercial Information Exchange)

Real estate agents and Real estate brokers

Banks (such as bank real estate owned departments for REO's and short sales)

Government entities (such as Fannie Mae, Freddie Mac and other government agencies)

Public auction (foreclosure sales, estate sales, etc.)

Private sales (transactions for sale by owner For sale by owner)

Real estate wholesalers and investors (flipping)

Once an investment property has been located, and preliminary due diligence (investigation and verification of the condition and status of the property) completed, the investor will have to negotiate a sale price and sale terms with the seller, then execute a contract for sale. Most investors employ real estate agents and real estate attorneys to assist with the acquisition process, as it can be quite complex and improperly executed transactions can be very costly. During the acquisition of a property, an investor will typically make a formal offer to buy including payment of "earnest money" to the seller at the start of negotiation to reserve the investor's rights to complete the transaction if price and terms can be satisfactorily negotiated. This earnest money may or may not be refundable, and is considered to be a signal of the seriousness of the investor's intent to purchase. The terms of the offer will also usually include a number of contingencies which allow the investor time to complete due diligence, inspect the property and obtain financing among other requirements prior to final purchase. Within the contingency period, the investor usually has the right to rescind the offer with no penalty and obtain a refund of earnest money deposits. Once contingencies have expired, rescinding the offer will usually require forfeiture of the earnest money deposits and may involve other penalties as well.

Sources of investment capital and leverage

Real estate assets are typically very expensive in comparison to other widely available investment instruments (such as stocks or bonds). Only rarely will real estate investors pay the entire amount of the purchase price of a property in cash. Usually, a large portion of the purchase price will be financed using some sort of financial instrument or debt, such as a mortgage loan collateralized by the property itself. The amount of the purchase price financed by debt is referred to as leverage. The amount financed by the investor's own capital, through cash or other asset transfers, is referred to as equity. The ratio of leverage to total appraised value (often referred to as "LTV", or loan to value for a conventional mortgage) is one mathematical measure of the risk an investor is taking by using leverage to finance the purchase of a property. Investors usually seek to decrease their equity requirements and increase their leverage, so that their return on investment (ROI) is maximized. Lenders and other financial institutions usually have minimum equity requirements for real estate investments they are being asked to finance, typically on the order of 20% of appraised value. Investors seeking low equity requirements may explore alternate financing arrangements as part of the purchase of a property (for instance, seller financing, seller subordination, private equity sources, etc.)

If the property requires substantial repair, traditional lenders like banks will often not lend on a property and the investor may be required to borrow from a private lender utilizing a short term bridge loan like a Hard money loan from a Hard money lender. Hard money loans are usually short term loans where the lender charges a much higher interest rate because of the higher risk nature of the loan. Hard money loans are typically at a much lower Loan-to-value ratio than conventional mortgages.

Some real estate investment organizations, such as real estate investment trusts (REITs) and some pension funds and Hedge funds, have large enough capital reserves and investment strategies to allow 100% equity in the properties that they purchase. This minimizes the risk which comes from leverage, but also limits potential ROI.

By leveraging the purchase of an investment property, the required periodic payments to service the debt create an ongoing (and sometimes large) negative cash flow beginning from the time of purchase. This is sometimes referred to as the carry cost or "carry" of the investment. To be successful, real estate investors must manage their cash flows to create enough positive income from the property to at least offset the carry costs.

Sources and management of cash flows

A typical investment property generates cash flows to an investor in four general ways:

net operating income (NOI)

tax shelter offsets

equity build-up

capital appreciation

Net operating income, or NOI, is the sum of all positive cash flows from rents and other sources of ordinary income generated by a property, minus the sum of ongoing expenses, such as maintenance, utilities, fees, taxes, and other items of that nature (debt service is not factored into the NOI). The ratio of NOI to the asset purchase price, expressed as a percentage, is called the capitalization rate, or CAP rate, and is a common measure of the performance of an investment property.

Tax shelter offsets occur in one of three ways: depreciation (which may sometimes be accelerated), tax credits, and carryover losses which reduce tax liability charged against income from other sources for a period of 27.5 years. Some tax shelter benefits can be transferable, depending on the laws governing tax liability in the jurisdiction where the property is located. These can be sold to others for a cash return or other benefit.

Equity build-up is the increase in the investor's equity ratio as the portion of debt service payments devoted to principal accrue over time. Equity build-up counts as a positive cash flow from the asset where the debt service payment is made out of income from the property, rather than from independent income sources.

Capital appreciation is the increase in market value of the asset over time, realized as a cash flow when the property is sold. Capital appreciation can be very unpredictable unless it is part of a development and improvement strategy. Purchase of a property for which the majority of the projected cash flows are expected from capital appreciation (prices going up) rather than other sources is considered speculation rather than investment.

CHAPTER EIGHTEEN

WAYS TO KICK-START YOUR CAREER IN REAL-ESTATE INVESTMENT

1. Don't wait for the right time.

Much like the stock market, in real estate we're always skulking and waiting, ready to pounce on what we believe is the perfect time to jump into the market. I'm here to tell you -- don't keep waiting. You can spend the next few years waiting for the perfect time, but if you have the startup funds and are eyeing a particular set of properties at a good deal, it's best not to wait.

Start out simple. Buy one or a few properties and go from there. The earlier you begin investing, the sooner your properties will begin to appreciate and, in turn, provide you with more capital to start your next venture.

2. Start bigger, sooner.

It's perfectly fine to begin investing in smaller, low-end properties -- but that's not how you build an empire. As soon as you have the hang of investing, don't hesitate when it comes to acquiring larger properties. Larger assets tend to appreciate faster and can be more beneficial to your portfolio as opposed to smaller, cheaper properties.

When considering if you should go big in real estate or return to the stock market, there are two more things to consider: 1)Properly investing in the stock market will cost you on average the same as investing in real estate, and 2) In real estate, even when the market crashes, you will still have a tangible asset to salvage. Of course, there are many other nuances when comparing the two, but to become a real estate mogul -- you'll have to stick to real estate.

3. Don't sell appreciating assets just yet.

When we're young, we tend to be quick to sell in hopes of making a return. This is the worst thing you can do in densely populated areas or up-and-coming cities. In these hot markets, the longer you wait to sell, the better. Across the country, in places like Seattle and Houston, many properties have doubled in value over the past three years.

Many of these properties will continue to appreciate, so determining when to sell is more complicated than simply seeing a slight return. Keeping track of market forecasts will help to determine when it's time to sell. This is also something that will be learned with experience.

4. Invest using a self-directed individual retirement account (IRA).

As an investor and entrepreneur, you should always be on the lookout for ways outside the obvious to improve your return. When using personal funds to invest, the best way to do it is through a self-directed IRA. A self-directed IRA is the same as the usual IRA, however, it allows alternative investments for your retirement savings. By investing through an IRA, you can avoid using your taxed income. Most banks have this option, so it's best to speak with a financial advisor before diving in head first with this kind of investment -- and remember to leave yourself with something for retirement.

Save yourself some trouble and remember these rules along with the basics when you're in the beginning stages of real estate investment. With so many details to consider, these simple rules can easily be overlooked.

CHAPTER NINETEEN

THE TIPS ENTREPRENEURS NEED TO KNOW BEFORE INVESTING IN REAL ESTATE

1. Do plan your financial goals.

Before you buy that first property, or do your first analysis, determine what you expect from your investments. What are your financial goals? We often discuss the "time vs. money" concept: The more you have of one, the less you need of the other to reach your financial goals. This means that you shouldn't shy away from taking the time to understand your goals and make sure each investment is a step toward achieving them. If you are unsure exactly how to create financial goals, meeting with a financial advisor is an excellent first step.

2. Don't spend a fortune on books, tapes and seminars, then just put all that information on a shelf.

You absolutely do need to learn some basics before venturing into investing. So, be sure to do some studying, but don't let "buying and collecting" information become your endgame. Again, having goals in mind will make the process much more straightforward. It's easy to get so tied up in the "research" phase that you never actually take action. Instead, write down specific questions you want answered or goals you want to meet before delving into the latest book/seminar/etc.

3. Do look at plenty of properties.

Don't just grab the first property you look at. Too many investors buy properties because they "look nice," or the investors don't want to put the work in to look at what's really out there. Remember, you won't be living there, so don't make your investment decision based on your personal preferences. While you shouldn't fall into the trap of analysis paralysis, make sure you are thorough in looking through properties. Give yourself a wide range of options, then narrow them down based on the criteria (goals) you have set for yourself.

4. Don't postpone starting your investment program because you're waiting for that perfect "unicorn" deal.

That's the flip side to number 3, of course. Plenty of beginning investors suffer from "a-better-deal-may-be-just-around-the-corner" syndrome. This can backfire in a big way, and you could potentially let a great deal slip just because you're holding out for something better. Your task may feel difficult if this is your first property, but you must realize that the "perfect deal" rarely (if ever) exists. Better to execute on a deal that meets most of your criteria than wait for another that may never come.

5. Do a thorough financial analysis.

Be realistic. Look at different alternatives to determine which makes the most financial sense. And never buy property at a higher price or on less attractive terms than your analysis says made sense. Be wary of sellers that try to over-estimate the value of the property through pro-forma (estimated) data. While you can certainly use a pro-forma to start the conversation, make sure you know the real numbers before closing. Look at previous years' tax returns, property-tax bills, maintenance records, etc. to get a good idea of the real income and expenses.

The most important figures you should know are:

Net income (income/expenses)

Cash flow (net income/debt financing payments)

Return on investment (cash flow/investment)

Cap rate (net income/property price)

Cash-on-cash return (cash flow/investment)

Total ROI (total return/investment)

In each case, "investment" refers to how much you invest in the property. "Debt financing" refers to any loans you may have to take out to buy the property. And "total return" refers to cash flow, equity accrual (i.e., equity gained from your tenants paying their rents), appreciation and taxes.

Once you have understood these figures, you should have enough information to determine whether or not acquiring the property fits with your financial goals.

6. Don't try to buy property that the seller is not motivated to sell.

If the seller is motivated to sell, you're not likely to get the price best aligned with your financial goals. So, how do you know if a seller is motivated? Look at the asking price. For example, If the property has been on the market for a year for, say, $200,000, with little-to-no price reduction, the seller is clearly not very motivated to move the property. However, if that same property has been on the market for a year and has had its price moved down considerably, the seller most likely wants to do whatever it takes to get the property off his or her hands. Of course, this raises the question of how to find motivated sellers. There are many approaches, and not all of these will work for you, depending on what property you want. But a few trusted methods include:

Attending open houses

Looking for vacant/unattractive properties that are for sale

Spreading the word about yourself and what properties you are looking for -- truly

Going the old-fashioned route and looking in the classifieds of your local paper

These are just a few ways to find sellers, but there are potentially dozens of other methods, depending on what type of property you're looking for.

7. Do know the difference between real estate investing and the business of real estate.

As an entrepreneur, you already have a business, and real estate investing is best used to support that business, not replace it -- unless that's your intention. In other words, don't get so caught up in executing transactions that your core business falters. If that happens, you'll be facing a bumpy road to get back to stability. Unless your business is itself real estate, or you're looking to get into the business full-time, always remember that pursuing these deals is a means to an end, not an end unto itself.

So, if you're interested in staying ahead of taxes and inflation while building security for the future, real estate investing may be for you. What are you waiting for?

CHAPTER TWENTY

THE WAYS REAL ESTATE INVESTORS MAKE MONEY

When you invest in real estate, there are several ways you can make money:

Real Estate Appreciation: This is when the property increases in value due to a change in the real estate market, the land around your property becoming scarcer or busier like when a major shopping center is built next door, or upgrades you put into your real estate investment to make it more attractive to potential buyers or renters. Real estate appreciation is a tricky game. In fact, it is riskier than investing for cash flow income.

Cash Flow Income: This type of real estate investment focuses on buying a real estate property, such as an apartment building, and operating it so you collect a stream of cash from rent, which is the money a tenant pays you to use your property for a specific amount of time. Cash flow income can be generated from well-run storage units, car washes, apartment buildings, office buildings, rental houses, and more.

Real Estate Related Income: This is income generated by "specialists" in the real estate industry such as real estate brokers, who make money through commissions from buying and selling property, or real estate management companies who get to keep a percentage of rents in exchange for running the day-to-day operations of a property. This type of real estate related income is easy to understand. For example, a hotel management company gets to keep 5% of a hotel's sales for taking care of the day-to-day operations such as hiring maids, running the front desk, mowing the lawn, and washing the towels.

Ancillary Real Estate Investment Income: For some real estate investments, this can be a huge source of profit. Ancillary real estate investment income includes things like vending machines in office buildings or laundry facilities in low-rent apartments. In effect, they serve as mini-businesses within a bigger real estate investment, letting you make money from a semi-captive collection of customers.

Tips for Purchasing Real Estate Investment Properties

There are several ways to buy your first real estate investment. If you are purchasing a property, you can use debt by taking a mortgage out against a property. The use of leverage is what attracts many real estate investors because it lets them acquire properties they otherwise could not afford. However, using leverage to purchase real estate can be dangerous because in a falling market, the interest expense and regular payments can drive the real estate investor into bankruptcy if they aren't careful.

You will almost NEVER purchase a real estate investment in your own name. Instead, for risk management reasons, consider holding real estate investments through special types of legal entities such as limited liability companies or limited partnerships (you should consult with a qualified attorney for his or her opinion as to which ownership method is best for you and your circumstances).

That way, if the real estate investment goes bust or someone slips and falls, resulting in a lawsuit, you can protect your personal assets because the worst that can happen in some circumstances is you lose the money you've invested. This lets you sleep at night because unless you've screwed up somewhere, your 401(k) plan assets, Roth IRA investment, and other retirement accounts should be out-of-reach.

Real Estate Investment: Types, Advantages & Disadvantages

In this lesson, we will explore different kinds of real estate investment properties. These types of properties include residential rental properties, commercial rental properties and 'flip' properties.

Property Investment

There are many types of property involved in real estate investing. Almost anyone can imagine buying a house but there are many other options to consider. Why invest in a house when you can invest in a duplex? What about investing in office buildings or warehouses? Do you want to be a landlord and collect rent or do you have a knack for finding 'fixer-upper' properties, repairing them and reselling them quickly for profit? Let's look at some different types of real estate investments and their advantages and disadvantages.

Residential Real Estate Rentals

The single family home is probably the first thing that comes to mind when someone imagines a real estate investment. The 'detached single family home' is the fancy real estate way of saying a typical American house. It is a house surrounded by a yard, driveway or sidewalk that isn't connected to somebody else's house.

Single family homes are just about everywhere and can be found at a variety of price points. These are the most desired types of housing by tenants. The volume of prospects make it possible for a savvy buyer to find a good deal. When trying to sell a single family home, many types of buyers may be interested. There are many financing programs and opportunities for investors to borrow money to make the purchase. However, single family homes can be expensive relative to the amount of income they generate for property investors. If the property goes vacant, there is zero rental income for an investor until a new tenant is found. It may take a long time to rent a single house.

Multi-family housing includes duplexes, triplexes and quadplexes. These homes have two, three or four units in one building, allowing up to four families to live on the same plot of land. Each unit is a unique rental opportunity. Because the units share walls, tenants will see and interact with their neighbors more than in a single family home but probably less so than if they lived in a large apartment building. Multi-family housing means multiple rent payers for a real estate investor. In a duplex, if one unit is vacant there could still be rental income from an occupied unit. If the owner lives in one of the units, an owner-occupied mortgage rate can be obtained.

This is cheaper than a commercial mortgage. Like single family housing, investors have many financing options. The multi-family market is often smaller than the single family home market. It may be more expensive to buy a four unit building than a single family house and if the investor sells the property, there will probably be fewer buyers.

Commercial Real Estate Rentals

Drive around town and what do you see? If buildings don't have someone living in them, they are probably commercial properties. Commercial real estate investments include office buildings, industrial buildings or even large apartment complexes. These buildings have benefits and challenges that differ from residential real estate. The tenants are generally going to be businesses rather than individuals. Rents might be negotiated in different ways from housing. For example, the rent could have scheduled increases over the life of the lease or be partially based on a percentage of sales. Commercial tenants are often more self-reliant than residential tenants and are more likely to stay for a longer duration than residential renters. Buyer qualification will depend less on the individual's income and more on the strength of the deal and the buyer's business qualifications. Commercial properties will require larger cash investments from the buyer. Commercial financing has different and more restrictive standards. In case of an economic downturn the property may sit vacant for years rather than a few weeks or months. There are fewer potential buyers compared to residential real estate.

CHAPTER TWENTY ONE

REAL ESTATE STATISTICS: WHY YOU SHOULD KNOW THE DATA

Do you know what's going on in your industry at a local and national level? Find out where to get statistics that give you a window into real estate, and how you can use those numbers to bring in more business.

Who's buying real estate in today's market? What are they really looking for? Why do for-sale-by-owners want to sell on their own? How many homes were actually sold through the assistance of a real estate professional?

These are just a few of the questions that statistics can answer for you. Fortunately, the NATIONAL ASSOCIATION OF REALTORS provides this research to its members on a regular basis. Having this information can help you become a better real estate professional, target your advertising to the right clientele, and aid in the preparation of reports and presentations.

If you don't take the time to get these facts, you're missing out on a wealth of resources that can help take your business to the next level. For instance, here are a few valuable stats from NAR's 2010 Profile of Home Buyers and Sellers:

The typical home buyer will search for homes for 12 weeks and view 12 different homes during the homebuying process.

83 percent of buyers purchased a home through a real estate agent.

48 percent of buyers found their agent through friend or family member.

The typical sellers lived in their homes for 8 years.

88 percent of sellers were assisted by an agent with their transaction.

Homes sold through a real estate agent sold for 96 percent of the list price.

57 percent of sellers reduced the asking price at least once while their home was listed.

The typical home is on the market for eight weeks.

86 percent of sellers surveyed were somewhat satisfied with their agent.

41 percent of sellers found the listing agent through a friend, family member, or coworker.

83 percent of consumers would definitely use their agent again.

How can this information help you and your business? Besides getting a better understanding of who today's consumer is, statistics can play a vital role with generating reports, presentations, and more.

Incorporate Local Statistics and Industry Trends

Being familiar with national data is important, but having stats on your local market is just as important, if not more so. Take the time to find out all you can about housing statistics in your own market area. Your multiple listing service can provide a wealth of info for you to share with consumers and news media services about what is going on in your own area.

You can also get a lot of good information from your local, regional, or state economic development agencies. Another excellent resource is www.census.gov, which has a vast library of data available for every county in the United States.

It's important for every real estate organization and practitioner to make sure their real estate Web site offers appropriate and relevant information. For example, first-time home buyers are becoming a bigger part of the market. If you want to work with them, your Web site should include more information about the homebuying process. According to NAR's 2010 Profile of Homebuyers and Sellers:

50 percent of recent home buyers were first-timers.

The typical first-time home buyer was 30 years old.

Repeat buyers were 49 years old on average.

One-third of recent home buyers indicated their primary reason for purchasing was a desire to own a home.

20 percent of recent home buyers were single females; 12 percent were single males.

Create Free Reports Downloads

Consumers love free stuff, and reports are no exception. Consider adding reports to your site that can help buyers and sellers during the transaction. For buyers, you might consider adding reports that include tips on buying a home and what they should do throughout the process. For sellers, you might add information about what they should do to prepare their home before selling as well as what they can expect during the contractual time frame. This type of information can help generate traffic to your Web site and build a resourceful library for consumers who want to learn more about buying and selling a home.

Produce and Upload Videos

Creating short videos about your company, the local marketplace, and information on buying and selling a home can play a key role in informing and attracting clientele. The videos also can give you exposure on larger sites like YouTube and Google, thereby increasing traffic to your site. Make sure that when you post videos to other Web portals, you use the appropriate tags and keywords to help consumers find them.

Two popular programs you can use to create educational videos about the homebuying process, statistics about your area, and general presentations are Jing and PowerPoint. With these two tools, you can easily convert your presentation into a video that you can post to your Web site or share on Facebook, YouTube, and Twitter.

Advertise to Target Markets

Advertisements, offerings of reports, and services should all be tailored to fit the needs of the consumers who are actively buying and selling real estate. As with any successful marketing strategy or campaign, you should take the time to think about how you can use the information to best reach your target market effectively.

Share Your Knowledge

As you begin to develop your knowledge of statistics in your market area, keep in mind that members of the local media will want to share that information with their audiences. This can be a win-win situation for everyone and create excellent public relations for you and your firm. Always be sure to give the appropriate credit for the sources you cite when working with the press. Also, including this information in postcards, advertisements, and general mailings to your sphere of influence can help portray you as the expert in your market.